FAULT LINE

Fault Line

LAURA LUSH

SIGNAL
EDITIONS

SIGNAL EDITIONS IS AN IMPRINT OF VEHICULE PRESS MONTREAL CANADA

Some of the poems in *Fault Line* first appeared or will appear in *The Antigonish Review, Dandelion, event, Poetry Canada Review, Vintage 91* and *96—Prize-Winning Poems from The League of Canadian Poets, The New Quarterly, Quarry, Prairie Schooner, The Southern Review, The South Carolina Review* and *Blues & True Concussions: Six New Toronto Poets* (Anansi).

I would like to thank both the Ontario Arts Council and the Toronto Arts Council for their generous support. Thank you also to Chris Wiseman, Lesley-Anne Bourne, Donna Burton, Michael Redhill, Curt Lush and, once again, to Michael Harris for bringing it all together.

Véhicule Press acknowledges the support of The Canada Council for the Arts for its publishing program.

Signal Editions Editor: Michael Harris
Cover art and design by J.W. Stewart
Photo of author by Curt Lush
Typeset in Perpetua by Simon Garamond
Printing by AGMV Marquis Inc.

Dépôt légal, Bibliothèque nationale du Québec and the
National Library of Canada, fourth quarter 1997

CANADIAN CATALOGUING IN PUBLICATION

Lush, Laura
Fault line

Poems.
ISBN 1-55065-096-3

I. Title

PS8573.U74F38 1997 C811'.54 C97-900982-0
PR9199.3L88F38 1997

Published by Véhicule Press, P.O.B. 125, Place du Parc Station,
Montreal, Quebec, Canada H2W 2M9
http://www.cam.org/~vpress

Distributed by General Distribution Services, Don Mills, Ontario M3B 2T6

Printed in Canada on alkaline paper.

CONTENTS

I FAULT LINE
Thaw 9
Garden 10
The Quiet 11
Morning Irises 12
Evening Irises 13
Hunter 14
Fault Line 15
October 16
Snow 17
Plants 18
Perennials 19
Children 20
The Last of Us 21
Genes 22
Dolly and Rose 23

II THE RAVINE
The Flyer 27
The Ravine 28
The Junk Man 30
Summer 31
My Mother's Voice 32
Pictures 33
The Hump 34
Runners 35
Victory 36
Barn 37
The Making of Rain 38
Fields 39
The House 40

III WASHIZU POEMS
Riverside Heights 43
Work 44
Joe 45
Gavey H 46

Gerry 47
Fluffy 48
Eugene 49
Kelly 50
The Session 51
Komachu's 52
Mama-san 53

IV DARKENING IN
Stars 57
Darkening In 58
Water 59
Firefly 60
Unrest 61
Border 62
Hook 63
Strays 64
Paperweight 65
Blue 66
River and Anger 67
Opal Moon 68

V THIS WOUND IS A FLOWER
Spring 71
Sky 72
Hunger 73
Samaritan 74
Lover 75
Mother Cave 76
Noah's Song 77
Loss 78
Morning 79
Blame 80
Fear 81
Song 82
Denial 83
Survival 84
Wound 85
Renewal 86

I

FAULT LINE

"Unreachable father, when we were first
exiled from heaven, you made
a replica, a place in one sense
different from heaven, being
designed to teach a lesson: otherwise
the same—beauty on either side, beauty
without alternative— Except
we didn't know what was the lesson."

—from *The Wild Iris*
Louise Glück

THAW

She tilts her ear to the small
confession of seeds

pulls at the ground
still frozen

her hands come up dark
the nails violent with spring

a raw sound of flowers
opening
winter tearing from a tree

a deep buried sound
thick as heart

those tiny strings that snap
as sky lets go of birds

these small deaths.

GARDEN

She moves among the rows discerning
the slender heft of asparagus,

the faint scent of peas. Snug in the pods,
small fetuses uncoil under her tongue.

Seeds pop between breaths.
Near her, the stillness of cows

steadying their bellies, teats slackening,
tame milk emptying into pails.

While birds, the colour of charred figs
wrap their wings in sun-splints.

THE QUIET

Give in. Surrender.

Let coals smoulder, pulling off the last bits of flames.
Follow the animals, their bodies ghosting the shades of trees.

Leave stealthily as Delilah holding crows of black hair.
Go. Go quickly as the lunar smell rushing over stone.

MORNING IRISES

Poling through reeds,
water shimmering with carp,
the sun a harpoon in our backs.
We dig softly, touch root, touch rock.
On either side, irises winged and swollen
like birds opening their glassy throats.

EVENING IRISES

The irises flicker
like tiny candles
afraid of their brightness.
They tug at the air—
soft, clear petals
tearing.
What do the irises do
but sigh in their violet profusion?
Their existence
a brief gold fire.
They float the garden,
disembodied spirits
dimming.

HUNTER

He presses his ear to the snow,
listens to moles chew back their shadows,
tails threading through dark.
Another five miles and the telephone poles vanish.
Just bush roaming bush.
There are things too small for his eyes—
bird scratches on ice,
old trails grunting with chase memories.
And this knife
like a wing of glass across its throat
as he cuts the doe warm,
the liver-smoothness when the hide opens.
His hands sink in deep,
twist like a cork, pull out the living strings—
a small heart, that one hooked jewel
glittering so blood-bright
in the wide miles of snow.

FAULT LINE

I have always loved you. It is true.
Your bitter crags, your fathomless lakes, your impossible deserts.
Even your billion-year-old suffering.
I'd gladly bear you again and again. I'd wrap myself in your wildfires,
your swamps, your sad man-woman thing.
I'd smooth your cracks, lick your wicked fault line,
again and again. Old Earth, I'd do all of this for you.
I lie awake at night just to listen to your dark plates'rubbing.
I am the dust of the tiny sepia rocks that wind flicks away.

OCTOBER

A thick sweater
we pull down
over our skins.

The only sound left—
of crickets igniting
their voices—a small
kindling of twigs.

Autumn comes toward us,
its night lamp lit.

Now tell me
what you want.

SNOW

It is the brief flash of deer.
It is the sky battening down the earth,
the long harsh spool of tundra
slowly unwinding.
It is the night breaking into its million star points.
It is flowers falling back into the garden,
a white fury of petals——
its complicated shroud
that only angels pass through.
It is the calm cold hand of God
closing the mouths of the dead.

PLANTS

My father holds the watering can,
lets go a small sprinkling.
Never too much or too little.
An expert at restraint.

He doesn't seem to mind
being needed, this being
depended on.

The plants venture nothing—
their voices locked in the small
fists of blooms.

They know they will be looked after.
Much like we knew we would be.
Even now, in our thirties,
we walk by him expecting to be fed,
waiting for that single drop of water.

PERENNIALS

With his knife he cuts a small country of grass,
shakes it like a rabbit's skin, loosening
the clumps of blood-dirt.
Then he cuts at the weeds, their difficult leaves.
He cuts with joy, with determination,
without fear that they will come back—which they surely will.

But it's the transplanting of the perennials.
How he lifts their slender noise, the buds' bright singing.
Then finds that one place for them to spill their seeds.

When he puts them into the ground,
a certainty comes back into the world—
that his line will continue
through these flowers,
these perennials' small exertings.
The roots already grabbing onto their tiny bit of earth,
these mother-strings.

CHILDREN

As my parents get older,
their memories form a blue viscous pond.
In the middle are us. Their children.
Small fish that nibble at the surface.
Sometimes we float on our backs
as if already surrendered
as if we won't get another chance.
It's hard to leave, harder to live.
We circle around each other,
each breath a link.
The underwater won't let us go
until we release our own eggs
like the tadpole, the salamander—
their awkward evolution
all blood and instinct.

THE LAST OF US

The ground pulls at our feet.
No small births burst back.
No roots grab. Instead, we roam
our small territories, careful
not to seed, not to build the nests too strongly.
We are surrounded by the half-glow
of rainbows, barely audible wings.
We are a gift no one can open.
Our hearts dry gourds in our chests.
If you approach, you will hear the warning
rattle. *Stay away.*

GENES

It lies coiled in the genes,
in the tightly sprung links of DNA,
the pink and blue locks of heredity.
You can see it in the slow
rotation of sockets, the silent struggle
of hips. It's waiting to work itself
through each generation. Slash
its gold tails. You'll recognize it instantly.
The way it reveals itself from brother to sister,
cousin to cousin.
It's the worm wriggling out of the apple,
a bright pearl of breath.
It's all the corners and walls.
The pitted skies.
It traps you with its continuity.
You would like to remove it from your body,
the way your mother removed the vein from the shrimp.
The knife making one quick incision,
that one delicate line gleaming with history.

DOLLY AND ROSE

Dolly and Rose. Rose and Dolly.
Together in their pink cottage
sitting on the verandah
drinking gin through straws
wondering every single evening
how all of a sudden
it got so dark. Their hair the same
shade of red when the sun glows
angry. The eyebrows arched
into teepees. Still laughing despite
the Parkinson's, mastectomies,
gout. Like to play cards—
blackjack, their red nails
covering the cards like tacks.
Old flappers that strung
hearts like beads. Their hands reach
into paper bags, pull out
Crown Royal—soft, amber and breathless.

II

THE RAVINE

THE FLYER

Stars, barely audible, stretch across the sky.
In the distance the Ferris Wheel turns,
the slowest of constellations.
I keep my money in a rabbit-skin pouch,
wrap the string around my hand. The very first place
is the Shell Tower. My father points and says, "Remember,"
as if it has already been hoisted
out of the debris of some war.
My sister and I run towards the great white
haunches of *The Flyer*,
its pronounced humps, its prehistoric stance.
While my brother walks towards the Freak House
where later Dainty Dora will lift her skirt,
offer loaf after loaf of white flesh.
It comes down to barely touching—
our heads skimming the height marker, the surly
attendant waving us on.
We pull the silver bar over our knees,
the car moves forward in slow caterpillar bumps.
Then *up, up*, the metal wheels tracking the chain,
the face of our father a small plate in the crowd.
Then the full forward thrust
of body and hair, our voices streaming ribbons.
The crowd below strangely still
as if they're the ones who've left this earth,
How does it feel? their eyes keep asking.
How does it feel to be up there while we are so safe
and lost down here?

THE RAVINE

We are nine and ten,
tiny brush strokes of legs,
arms that have just wrapped around
the world for the first time.

Down to the ravine
past the waning stench of winter,
the trees locked in their
death-scents.

We run past
the numbed buds
the white mouths of icicles
shiny as fish.

See the white houses
that brick our dreams every night.
The unflowing river.
How its water has stopped for us,
hardened like our brothers' penises.
With our skateblades
we unstitch the ice,
split the pond's underbelly.

We are girls
so we wait for blood
while our mothers
swell in their ageing pods.

We hook our young bodies
into the cold, against each other
while the two dogs entwine.
The thick bud where their bodies meet.

The female is always the first to pull away,
neck hair raised, the back legs
the most vulnerable of bows.

Towards the pond she runs
as we hold the male back
by the scruff—
their history a brief flash of snow.

We wait for her soft-padded retreat—
the long thin blade of her bark
that signals she's safe.

THE JUNK MAN

He lived next door.
The wide chrome smile,
the lawn that shook like
a rusty dog. Afternoons
gleaming bright as bumpers
as the dragon-flies hovered
over old toilet bowls
in delicate tremors.
How he'd walk between
the shells of cars,
pass them quietly
as if they were sleeping,
as if their tires
were still weary with roads.

SUMMER

Between the rows of corn, the gold pronouncements
of summer, we lie on the earth on our backs.

Tiny vagrants alone in our bodies.
Ragged children who have strayed from our homes.

Nothing insurmountable—the warm wet passageway
to the underground fort.

On either side, the earth moving its cow belly.
Slow song of grass yellowing.

The boys' crude beds of stones and twigs. Pyres
that later sink into the ground.

All of this to keep us away from the small pouch of marbles—
the limed eyes of dead birds glowing off sticks.

All things transfixed:
the chrysalides' luminous quiet, the stars' rubied prayers.

De-winged, leaves jostling across the sky.

What's left?

Our bodies, the axis under the weight of copper sky.
Our belief that all things begin from our hands,

that even summer can be contained in a jar—
the one butterfly bright enough to last past autumn.

As our heads keep turning with the blue curve of earth
pulling legs, arms toward the fantastic rush of our lives.

MY MOTHER'S VOICE

My mother's voice is a perfect arrow.
It just comes out straight and direct.
Especially when there is bad news.
It is as if some doctor has anesthetized her spirit,
has made her heart somehow less red,
less alive.
Not like my sister whose lungs
are made of glass.
Words break through her body.
You can hear the air shatter
when she speaks.

I am more like my mother:
I can force the arrow upward
from the heart
without taking any blood,
without puncturing any flesh.
With our voices, my mother and I,
we can pass through anything.
Even grief. Even joy.
Each other. Ourselves.

PICTURES

In pictures, they are different people.
They stand with their arms around each other.
They smile into the still blue eye of the camera.
They are Siamese twins before the separation
enjoying the last bond of flesh.
And when the flash is over,
they do separate.
Miraculously.
Without blood or tearing.
He, back to the garden.
She, to the kitchen.
Whatever connection there was between them is lost
until the photos appear.
Everything intact except themselves.

THE HUMP

When I give my father a backrub,
I navigate his life—the victories,
the lingering ache
of every vertabrae.

It's the only thing I can give him—
my hands on his back.

At the base of his neck
I find the hump.
We all have one:
some sort of creature we carry
on our backs, more dead than alive,
more pit than fruit.

I pour the oil over the hump,
gloss its small hill, smooth
its incongruity, its stubborn arch.

Even when I press down, try
to shape the hump into something different,
it becomes more persistant.
Like all his unborn
children trying
to push forth.

RUNNERS

I know why my father
got married, had children.
He wanted to slough off some
of the fatigue,
the way his own father rid
himself of his battle scars. Lay them
like wreaths over each child.
The minute our heads appeared,
he knew things would be different.
He knew we wouldn't have to struggle as hard
or for as long.
Our breaths already in us.
Our veins filled with his powerful
blood-force.
To him, we had already run marathons.
Now all we had to do was live.

VICTORY

Each year he adds another one
to his body, arranges the dark plum
buds so they are far from all the vital parts:
the heart, the groin, the small residue of soul.
Then he lifts his legs, the ones that carried
him through marathons, sales meetings,
the blue rooms of domesticity.
Walks toward one more day, its tentative sun,
its tumorous clouds.
He walks past the hecklers, the disbelievers,
the cynics.
He walks past the hopeless, the malcontents,
the browbeaters.
And says nothing.
Only keeps walking until the small buds
around his neck burgeon as if they were a garland of laurels—
as if, at last, he's finally crossed the line.

BARN

The door opens.
My father enters
in his red plaid jacket.
His hands kneading
the bellies of cows.

All winter, waiting
for swallows to press their wings
across a moment of sun.

In the corner, a sow turns
to farrow.

Twenty years later
he wakes up,
the barn empty.
Rubs his hands across wood,
old shadows.

THE MAKING OF RAIN

First there was sky and the vast panic
of emotions that filled the sky.
Then the trees reached up, rubbed their leaves a bit
and slowly the sky became a little un-dark, lifting
its solemness like a man, too long on this earth,
lifts his hands away from his face—
all for the sake of this tiny bit of light, this sun-rope.
But the geese grabbed the rope,
flung it like a long yellow snake until the sky
burst into bits of rain.

FIELDS

I lie in these fields
ribbed with the thousand-thick bones
of groundhogs, gophers.
The snakes' fine skeletons
necklaced around rocks.
The quarry mounds,
Indian burial grounds my brother says.
And the fields are holy.
And the fields do drum their stones
heavy with grace.

THE HOUSE

My father bought my mother
another house,
hung it from the branch,
the one by the window, *the baking window.*
It's her little bit of reprieve. This house—
the one outside—bright orange, bird-visited
by cardinals, jays, even the timorous ghosts of humming-birds.
They flutter their wings against the window.
But they don't visit the house she's in.
The kitchen floor has a hold of her legs, feet.
She's sinking. She's sinking.

III

WASHIZU POEMS

(Washizu is a small town bordering Lake Hamana in Central Japan)

RIVERSIDE HEIGHTS

It was as if some giant had landed there years before
and, from his pocket, placed the little blue house
down on the grass, fresh and shiny as an after dinner mint.
And the house sat there for a little while
until they came—these Irish—all seven of them,
dragging the tattered cloth of their own island behind them,
and stuffed their too-big bodies into those too-small rooms
with the too-small beds that shook every time a train rattled past.
They didn't know then that they were making local history,
that for years after their departure,
the neighbours would still be talking about *them.*
How their windows and balconies flowered with dirty laundry,
how their boxers sailed from the TV antennae regally as kites.
How on Friday nights—or sometimes even Tuesdays—they'd run
up and down the stairs banging pots—and still later,
home after the pub, they'd charge through each other's flats
with *kendo* sticks and boogie boards, mad as bulls.
It was presumed on many a night that they had killed one other,
squashed each other's bodies into wardrobes
and garbage bags, tossed them off the balcony
into the clear shimmering of rice paddies.
While their fortress slowly grew—the tall brown
beer bottles, toppling one after the other
like fallen soldiers.
Some nights
they still see them dancing.
The white-bellied pagans from another kind of island.

WORK

Heigh Ho! Heigh Ho! Off to work
they *didn't* go, never went.
Went back to the flat to watch a video.
Or surfed.
Or stayed in bed for an extra long shag.
Or stayed in bed.
Or went for a drive to the Circle K,
to the beach, *anywhere*.
Or they sat in the jakes and read the paper.
Or just sat in the jakes.
Or went to the canteen to sneak a cup of coffee.
Or downstairs—upstairs—back down again.
Or sometimes they just stood on their desks
and thumped on their chests until all the wires
and parts and grommets and connectors
finally burst through their bellies.
Until they were young and pure once again,
before this, before *work* ruined them.

JOE

Was the only one who kept
fresh bread, kept *anything*.
Did his washing, paid his bills,
cooked, scrubbed and cleaned,
busked and sang,
scrounged and saved—spent none.
Joe was the only one who was on time,
on the ball, on the run
from the rest of *them*.

GAVEY H.

Because he had big blondie curls
and a wrinkly sprog face.
Because he had the mouth of a Cork boy,
the Yoda ears, the laugh of a million
churlish children.
Because he was the only one who
could *get away with it,* could *get away,* could *get it,*
they all wanted to kill him.
But he left.

GERRY

Actor, orator—pontifical
pugilist of words.
Hell-bent on arguing the stars
from the sky.
And all the girls fancied him—
Yeats's younger perfect cloth.

FLUFFY

Wasn't from this place we call earth.
No he wasn't.
He had a way of looking up
like a pointer
waiting for that bird to finally
drop from the sky.

EUGENE

Head lowered into a bowl of *ramen*
or in between your breasts.
That inimitable bristly-haired,
calf-eyed, slack-mouthed,
Say-yeh-love-me-Eugene.

KELLY

Think white shirt, hair cut short.
Destroyer grin.
And that's all you need to know.

THE SESSION

During the week, they roamed the flat
tense and lithe as greyhounds.
These were their days of rest. Misfit knights
preparing for a great battle.
They slept naked, woke the next day
with all the old parts miraculously intact—
the hands working the air, the knees bending
back and forth as they pushed through the day, heads lowered,
struggling to get back to the place
before their bodies had clogged and died.
And when the five o'clock bell rang, they ran and ran
and kept running until they were on the 9:36 train
with skins wet and shiny. And finally they
were there—bursting through the bar—*seven, seventeen, seventy*
thick as Marlboro looked up,
issued his *I-ras-shai-ma-se's*.
Then Joe and Brian would bring out their guitars.
And in walked the babes! *Jaysus the babes!*
Maura and Christina, Jan and Heidi.
Donna, Mi-La and Kristyn. And your ones
from Iwata. And your ones from Hamamatsu
who still glowed like nice new ones do.
Then beer after beer being passed swiftly as batons
while the others tumbled in, red-faced, ready.
Mecca and Colin, Shanley and Seanie. Pearce, Aido and Tom.
Ha Ha Connors with his mickey of whiskey under his coat.
The race still on—Friday pushing into Sunday
where only the fit and few will survive.

KOMACHU'S

It was our second home. And our Mama
fed us. Oh how she fed us well.
Tsukaemono, takenoko, yakitori.
It was our little masked bar,
our laughing room, our cheering room,
our place of solitude and a kind of winter
holiness that battens the memory forever.
It was our chapel, our temple, our little red-roofed
sky. Our spring, summer, fall, winter.
It was the first unravelling—the veil off the face.

MAMA-SAN

First you pass through the beads in the doorway.
You bend your head a little. You wait for Rieko-san
to rush at you with her hot little towels,
for Mama-san to clear the side of the bar for you.
You have special gifts. Things she has never seen before.
She will change the menu, add cream corn and spuds.
She will watch over your slow, strange growing in her country.
She will watch you edge your way into love and out of it again.
Another one of your magic tricks.

IV

DARKENING IN

"Women and men (both dong and ding),
summer autumn winter spring,
reaped their sowing and went their came
sun moon stars rain."

—e.e. cummings

STARS

The stars appear one by one
like small songs,
like small terrors
rattling bright in their cages.

The moon so skin.
Pale rice paper
awash in moon-blood.

The wolf—
a brilliant blue flame
through the trees.

DARKENING IN

Winter and the air shines.
The smallest of stars barely breathing.
Birds unfold their wings,
fly their smooth-sounding flights.
Watch them blurring past,
white stains on the night.
They see the forest turning,
trees darkening in
for night, for life.

Later,
a man undoes the world,
his wife's hair.
He waits patiently—
like a husband, like a hostage.
Waits till she frees the day
from him.

Love, a small drink
of cold lake
he cannot get enough of,
cannot jump in
or out of
quickly enough.

WATER

Picture the moon finally free
hurtling through the sky
calm and clear as stone.
The long cool blades of grass
folding over your face like a praying mantis.
What the water does is not so sad.
The fish rub the riverbed with rock-flayed bellies.
They push through the water
knowing that their bodies
are underwater knives
that cut through nothing.
Their suffering born again and again.
Water is the cold hard pressing
down of memory on fish.

FIREFLY

What small lit secret
are you trailing through the dark?
What small warning
are you leaving in the trees?
Or are you simply signaling
the end of berries
now so dry and acrid on the bear's tongue?

UNREST

After a while
you get comfortable

listening to your
blood pass over your bones.

The love and hate
battling every cell.

If only alone didn't
mean peace.
And together unrest.

BORDER

Do you see the gold filigrees of light?
Do you know they are still selling roses
in Warsaw, drinking the cool blue
streams of vodka?
After three years you still
don't know how to step back
into your country. You dream its border.

What good would it do
to wake you?
Whiskers rising like tiny
black whips on your face.
How is it that you look so peaceful
yet wake with your head in your hands?

HOOK

No matter how far
I am away from you,
I can still see
you lying on the bed
like a fresh-caught fish,
the hook
still lodged.
You can't blame
me for the
rip.
Life did that. Not me.
I only pulled you in.
I only pulled you in.
Now breathe.

STRAYS

I used to bring home strays:
cats with one ear, no tails.
I was convinced that love
could make a difference.
But there was something
permanent in their bodies
that sent them flying out of my hands
no matter how gently
I held them,
no matter how often
I reassured them.
It is how I flee
a man's grip today,
squirming away whenever
he tries to hold me.
I am a fish
flopping between
his fingers, my one eye
gelatinous, gold.
It is all in the body
my latest lover tells me.
It is all in the way
we have learned about abandonment
and then to abandon.

PAPERWEIGHT

You set your heart down on mine.
A bloody paperweight, heavy with
somebody else's grief—not mine.
No wonder I'm tired.
No wonder I can't put one foot
in front of the other.
I will stay like this for years
until I finally learn to slip away—
a dark shiny page falling
to the floor.

BLUE

If I had to do it again,
I would bite my own umbilical cord.
I would stop the rivers
of mother in my own body.

I would wrestle
the seed
under—
its conifer head splitting.

I would spit out all
the faulty wires,
the chipped genes.

I would peel my many skins,
return to the pond,
its deep amphibian blue.

RIVER AND ANGER

The river is sure and so it surges
forward, tumbles salmon like dice.
We sit on the banks watching.
Our bodies give off nothing.

We would like to be that powerful,
to be current, eddy, this colossal water.
But we are not like the river.
Our breaths small dark beads.

Yet we still push our small fish-lives
upstream. We covet our eggs.
Especially the eggs.
Perfect blood-drops
buried under riverbed.

Only the river can keep them safe.
Only the river can give them back
to the world trembling on every surface.

OPAL MOON

Opal Moon,
beatific moon.

Bigamist among
the shuddering stars.

Carry this old earth,
cradle the lakes and trees.

Rub your mint throat across deer.

Come quickly, come quietly,
the animals are retreating.

The fox, the hare, the speckled bands
of snakes. Slowly, slowly,
undulating south.

V

THIS WOUND IS A FLOWER

"There is no other memory other than the memory of wound."

—Czeslaw Milosz, Nobel Prize Lecture, 1980

SPRING

It is April and the small-bodied cherries
cling to the trees like suicide attempts.
Just the same, the couples are in love
and quite unaware of these.
They only see the sky wide and opening,
the flowing stitches of birds.

SKY

What wing tore
the sky from you?
Now bunched like
a red handkerchief
in my hands.

HUNGER

If I could I would lay
my mouth over yours.
Suck the blood quiet.
All night, my lips
supping on grief.

SAMARITAN

I carried you that night,
even though your body wasn't in my arms.
Instead—a hovering, a mothed knife
flitting around my wrists.
While she—the dark-eyed one—gave you tea,
stitched you—thread by thread—shut.

LOVER

As you lay in bed,
your body floated above
the talk of lilies.
Girls, drunkenly, called your name.
I peeled your shadow from you,
wrapped it around my body.
Like a lover,
like love's hot poultice.

MOTHER CAVE

The dark
lopes back home.
My mother cave comes
clean. Spooled tight, bone
flaying bone. You fold into me.
Difficult origami
with your steel-honed wings.

NOAH'S SONG

For two long weeks,
I watch your body swell
like the heaviest of oceans.
With it, it takes everything
I've ever known: the ribbed wind,
the slow tug of sky.
With my tongue, crimson paddle,
I crush the words between my teeth.
All night I build my shore
of sullen songs.

LOSS

Something is gone now.
Mostly my belief that nothing can
ever happen to you.
You want me to walk you through the thorns,
pass your body like a lamp through the dark.
Small stars live in your veins.
They keep the blood warm.
The blood warm still.

MORNING

The sun opens like a cobra.
Spits gold, flecks of heat
over field, valley.
The birds glitter like small hooks
cloven to a too-blue sky
that I puzzle together
drop by drop.

BLAME

Knowing who did it
wouldn't change anything.
Especially why.
The feet only knowing
this way or that way,
stone or marsh.
Not the paths, serpentine,
rising up
through the dark.

FEAR

After, everyone wanted
to know what happened.
Especially the children
with their night-bereft eyes.
They held candles up to your face,
watched your irises eat
their small trails of fear.

SONG

The wound sings differently
today. Ripples across your face
like the first light.
Don't look.
Instead, touch.
Just touch all the new
black and blue parts.

DENIAL

I have my back to you.
Smooth and cold
as a stone.
You press yourself
against what will never
reach out—the heart
a thing of resistance, a shudder of wall.
Love, the only irrefutable thing.

SURVIVAL

You have what you must.
I have what lies between us—
a small bloody animal
you refuse to name.   Watch me
push and pull,
push and pull
the silence from you.

WOUND

This wound is too deep for both of us.
Not a broach or a button of flesh
that you can undo at night.
But something permanent,
a third eye that wavers
in its knowing.
Ask the dark, it'll tell you what happened.
Some mornings shining up red and opulent
as an apple that you handpicked
from a farmer's field.
If you were ten, you would be hero
with your boy-track of scars.
But as a man
the wound lies barely
open like the barely opened eyes of a prisoner.
For the first time,
you search for me,
my small kisses that riddle your body.

RENEWAL

Listen,
if I could make you see colour,
you would rise again
like a beautiful spring crocus.
You would unpin
your arms from the sky,
suck the small holes
in your hands
until the wounds
hissed shut.
You would drink cup after
cup of sweet milk
mistake it for my own.
If I could make
you see colour, you would pluck
your own heart,
peel it like a plum.
And taste and taste.

Signal Editions Poetry Series

edited by Michael Harris

SELECTED POEMS David Solway
THE MULBERRY MEN David Solway
A SLOW LIGHT Ross Leckie
NIGHT LETTERS Bill Furey
COMPLICITY Susan Glickman
A NUN'S DIARY Ann Diamond
CAVALIER IN A ROUNDHEAD SCHOOL Errol MacDonald
VEILED COUNTRIES/LIVES Marie-Claire Blais
Translated by Michael Harris
BLIND PAINTING Robert Melançon
Translated by Philip Stratford
SMALL HORSES & INTIMATE BEASTS Michel Garneau
Translated by Robert McGee
IN TRANSIT Michael Harris
THE FABULOUS DISGUISE OF OURSELVES Jan Conn
ASHBOURN John Reibetanz
THE POWER TO MOVE Susan Glickman
MAGELLAN'S CLOUDS Robert Allen
MODERN MARRIAGE David Solway
K. IN LOVE Don Coles
THE INVISIBLE MOON Carla Hartsfield
ALONG THE ROAD FROM EDEN George Ellenbogen
DUNINO Stephen Scobie
KINETIC MUSTACHE Arthur Clark
RUE SAINTE FAMILLE Charlotte Hussey
HENRY MOORE'S SHEEP Susan Glickman
SOUTH OF THE TUDO BEM CAFÉ Jan Conn
THE INVENTION OF HONEY Ricardo Sternberg
EVENINGS AT LOOSE ENDS Gérald Godin
Translated by Judith Cowan
THE PROVING GROUNDS Rhea Tregebov
LITTLE BIRD Don Coles
HOMETOWN Laura Lush
FORTRESS OF CHAIRS Elisabeth Harvor
NEW & SELECTED POEMS Michael Harris
BEDROCK David Solway
TERRORIST LETTERS Ann Diamond
THE SIGNAL ANTHOLOGY Edited by Michael Harris
MURMUR OF THE STARS: SELECTED SHORTER POEMS Peter Dale Scott
WHAT DANTE DID WITH LOSS Jan Conn
MORNING WATCH John Reibetanz
JOY IS NOT MY PROFESSION Muhammad al-Maghut
Translated by John Asfour and Alison Burch
WRESTLING WITH ANGELS: SELECTED POEMS Doug Beardsley
HIDE & SEEK Susan Glickman
MAPPING THE CHAOS Rhea Tregebov
FIRE NEVER SLEEPS Carla Hartsfield
THE RHINO GATE POEMS George Ellenbogen
SHADOW CABINET Richard Sanger
MAP OF DREAMS Ricardo Sternberg
THE NEW WORLD Carmine Starnino
THE LONG COLD GREEN EVENINGS OF SPRING Elisabeth Harvor
FAULT LINE Laura Lush